imagine

Juan Felipe Herrera   illustrated by Lauren Castillo

CANDLEWICK PRESS

IF I PICKED chamomile flowers
as a child
in the windy fields and whispered
to their fuzzy faces,

imagine

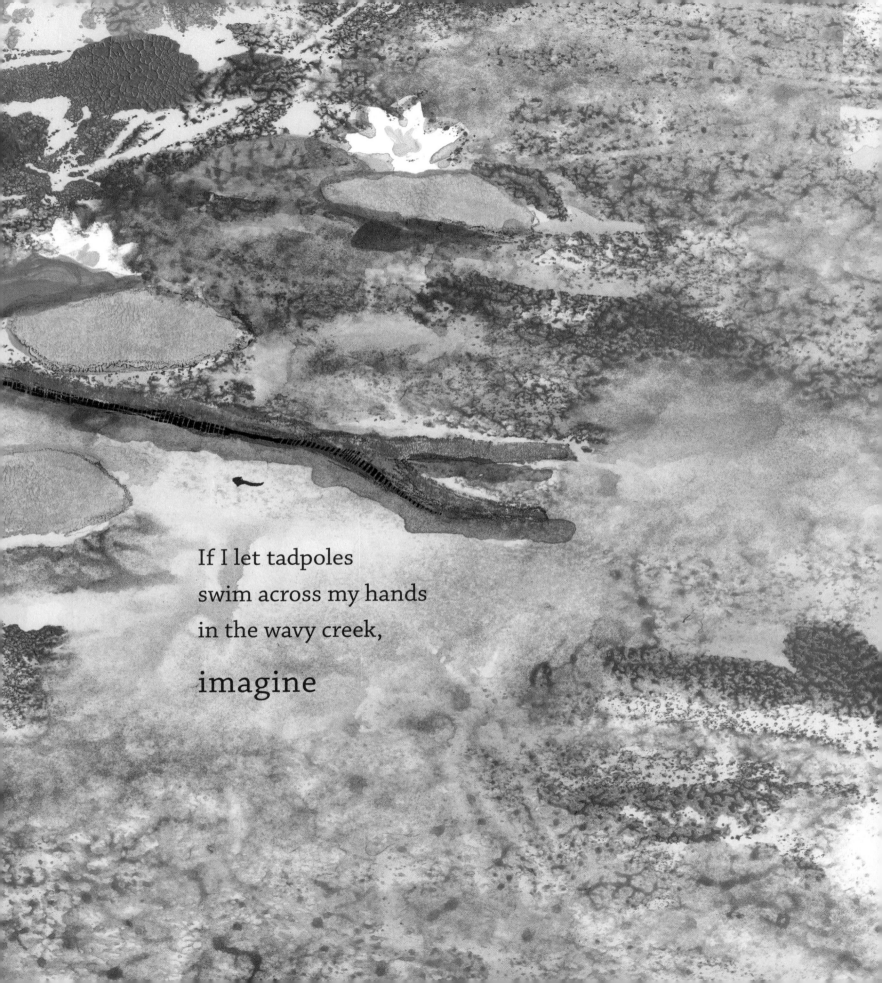

If I let tadpoles
swim across my hands
in the wavy creek,

imagine

If I jumped up high
into my papi's army truck
and left our village of farmworkers
and waved adios
to my amiguitos,

imagine

If I let the stars
at night
paint my blanket with milky light
with shapes of hungry birds
while I
slept outside,

imagine what you could do . . .

If I helped Mamá
feed the hopping chickens
and catch the crazy turkey
in the front yard
of our new village,

imagine

If I walked
through the evening forest
at the top of a mountain
with a silvery bucket
to fetch water
from the next town,

imagine

If I moved
to the winding city
of tall, bending buildings
and skipped
to a new concrete school
I had never seen,

imagine

If I opened
my classroom's wooden door
not knowing how to read
or
speak in English,

imagine

If I practiced
spelling words
in English by
saying them in Spanish
like — pehn-seel for
pencil,

imagine

If I collected gooey and
sticky
ink pens because
I loved how the ink flowed
like tiny rivers across
soft paper,

imagine

If I grabbed a handful
of words
I had never heard and
sprinkled them over a paragraph
so I could write
a magnificent story,

imagine

Choir

tortillas

little chicks

Papá Felipe

pollo

Mamá Lucha

beans

frying pan

school

guitar

songs

If I stood up
in a school far away from
where I lived
and sang
for the first time
in front of class,

imagine

If I started to write
a poem
on a skinny paper pad after school
as I walked on the wide sidewalk
and then finished it
when
I got home,

imagine

If I picked up
my honey-colored guitar
and called out my poem
every day
until it turned into a
song,

imagine

the road

poema

rainbow

comal

If I gathered
many words and many more songs
with both of my hands
and let them fly
over my mesa
and turned them into a book
of poems,

imagine

luna

Río

chamomile

radio

la tarde

If I stood up
wearing a robe
in front of my familia and many more
on the high steps
of the Library of Congress
in Washington, D.C., and
read out loud and signed
my poetry book
like this—
Poet Laureate of the United States of America

imagine what you could do.

For Anthony, Cyrus, Dominic, Dylan, Felix, Gianna,
Kimiko, Kaito, Lucas, Luna, Paloma, Solana, and Tanner.
And in memory of my sister, Sara Chavez.
J. F. H.

For Alanna.
And for all dreamers.
L. C.